Tembo, Twiga, and Friends
AFRICAN ANIMALS

By Susan Szymczyk Craig

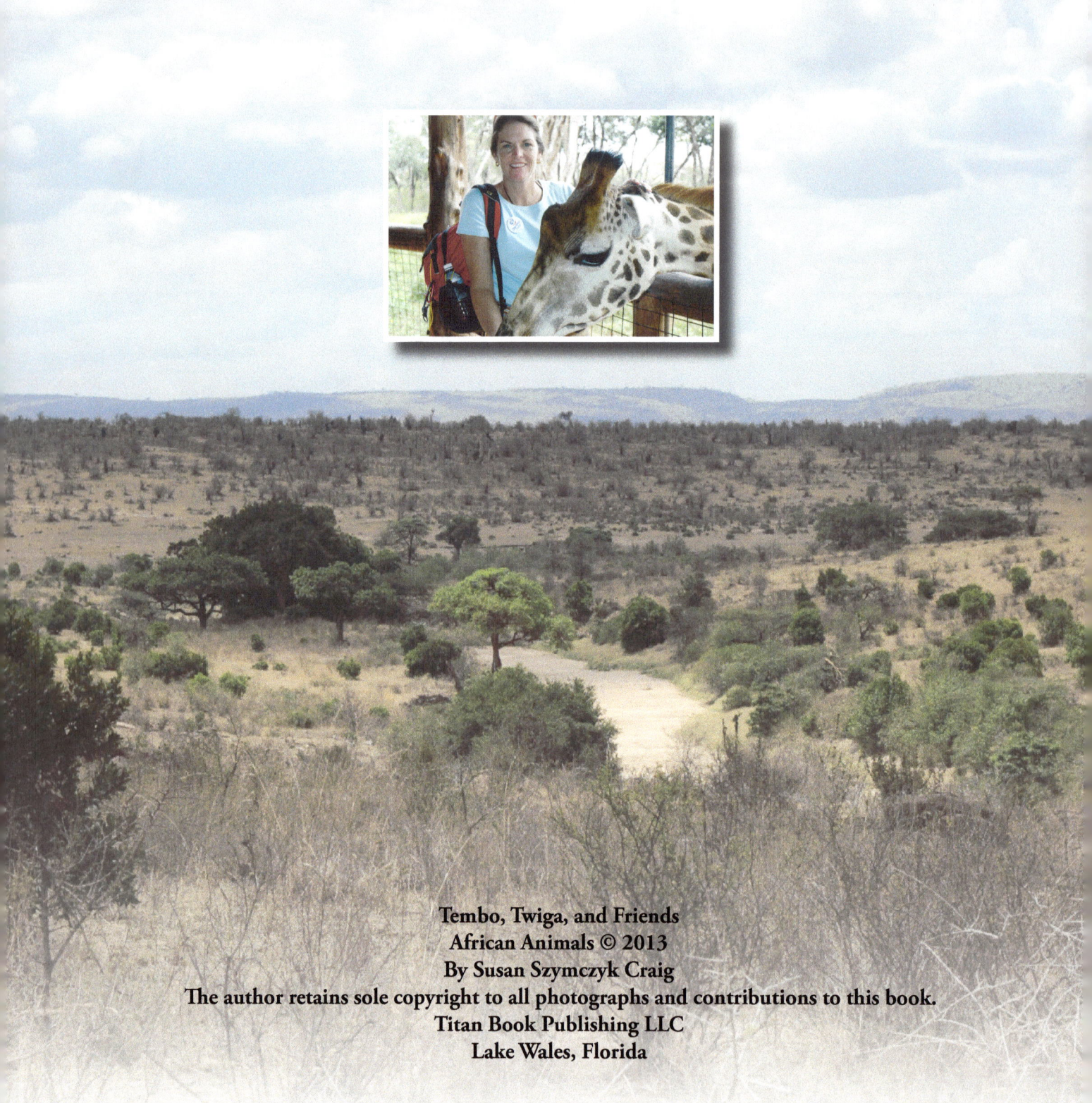

Tembo, Twiga, and Friends
African Animals © 2013
By Susan Szymczyk Craig
Titan Book Publishing LLC
Lake Wales, Florida

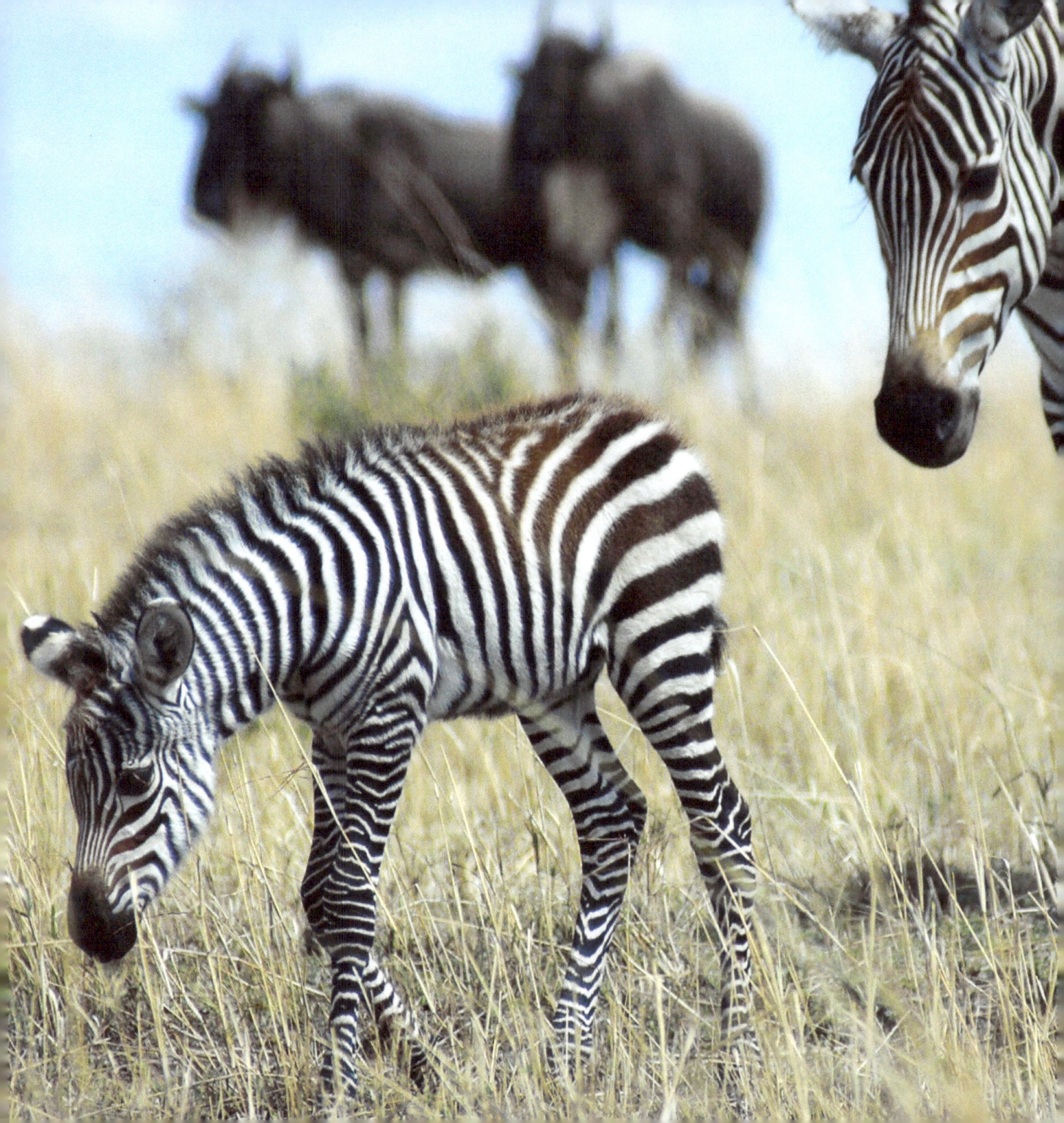

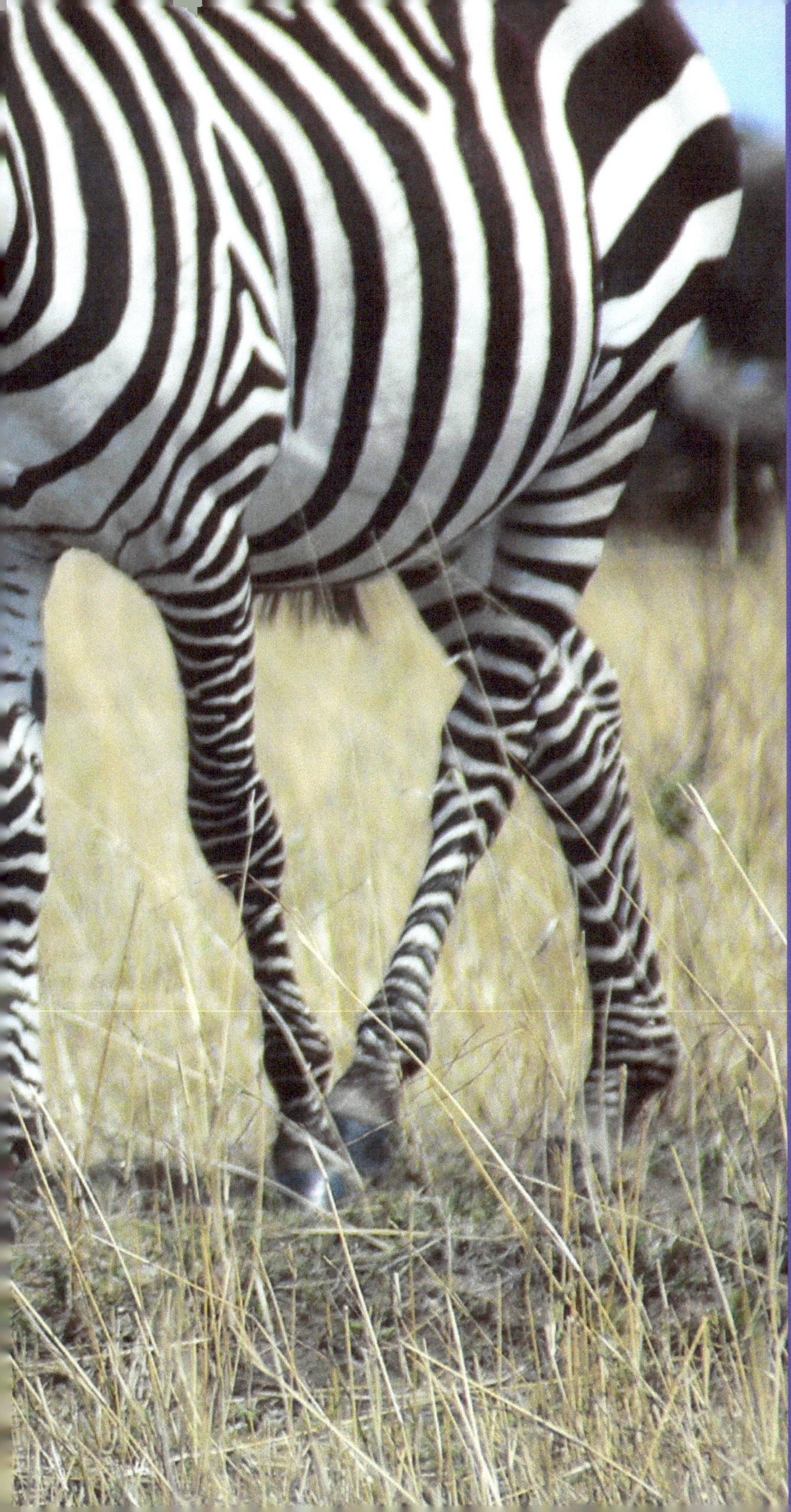

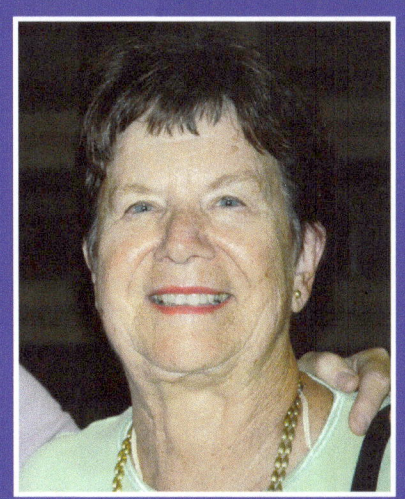

This book is dedicated to:

Katharine Lloyd-Rees Miller

I am eternally grateful to Katharine for introducing me to Operation Smile and for insisting that I accompany her to the Masai Mara, Kenya on Safari in November 2006 after completing our medical mission in Nairobi. Katharine has been my mentor, my teacher, my Aunty, and most importantly, my friend.

I have created this book to share my pictures with my niece, Daisy, my great nephews, Harrison and Henry, cousin Roy, as well as anyone else who will appreciate the beautiful animals found in the wilds of East Africa.

Susan Szymczyk Craig 2012

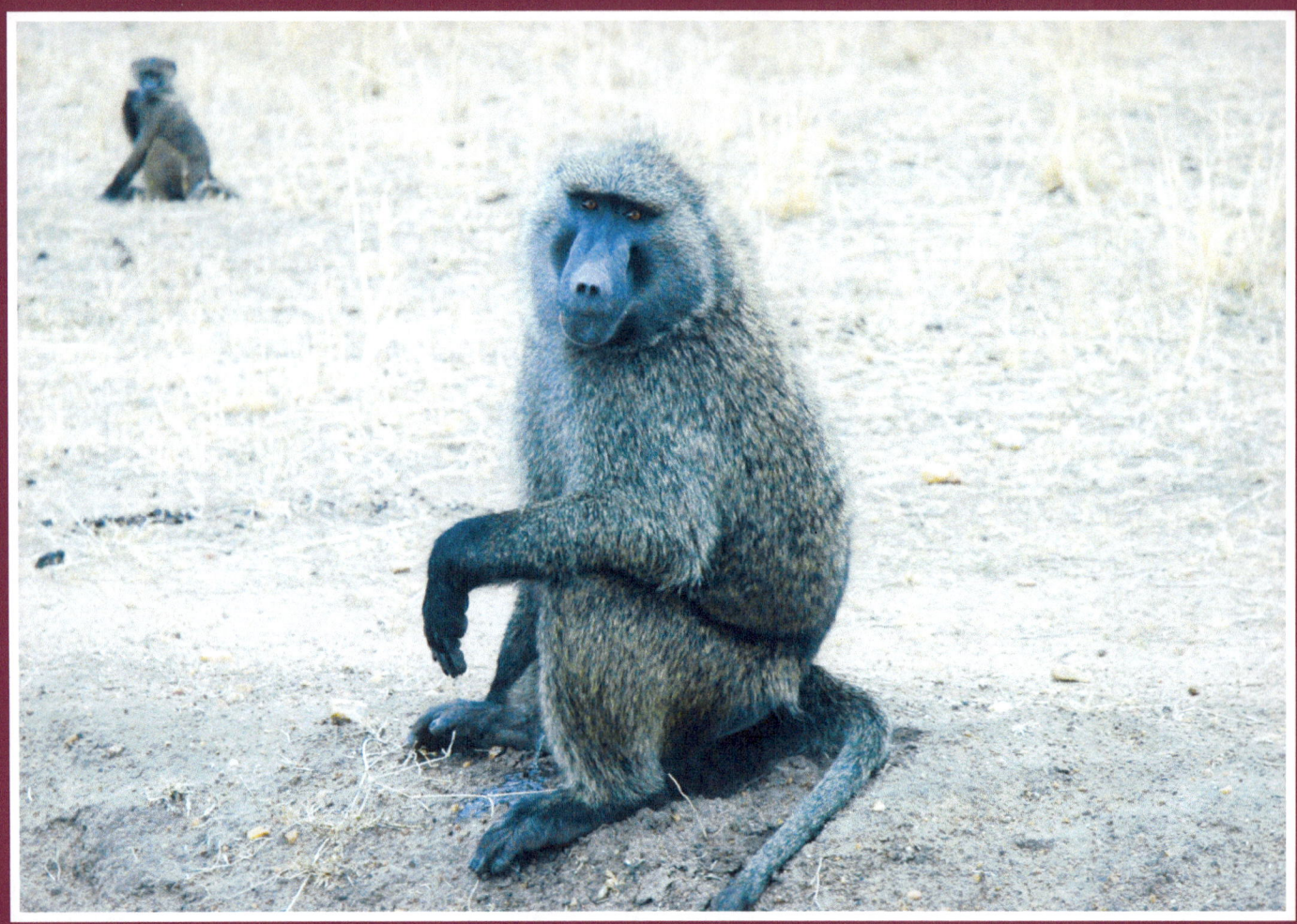

Baboon

狒狒	Babouin	Pavian	Babbuino	Babuino	Nyani
Chinese	French	German	Italian	Spanish	Swahili

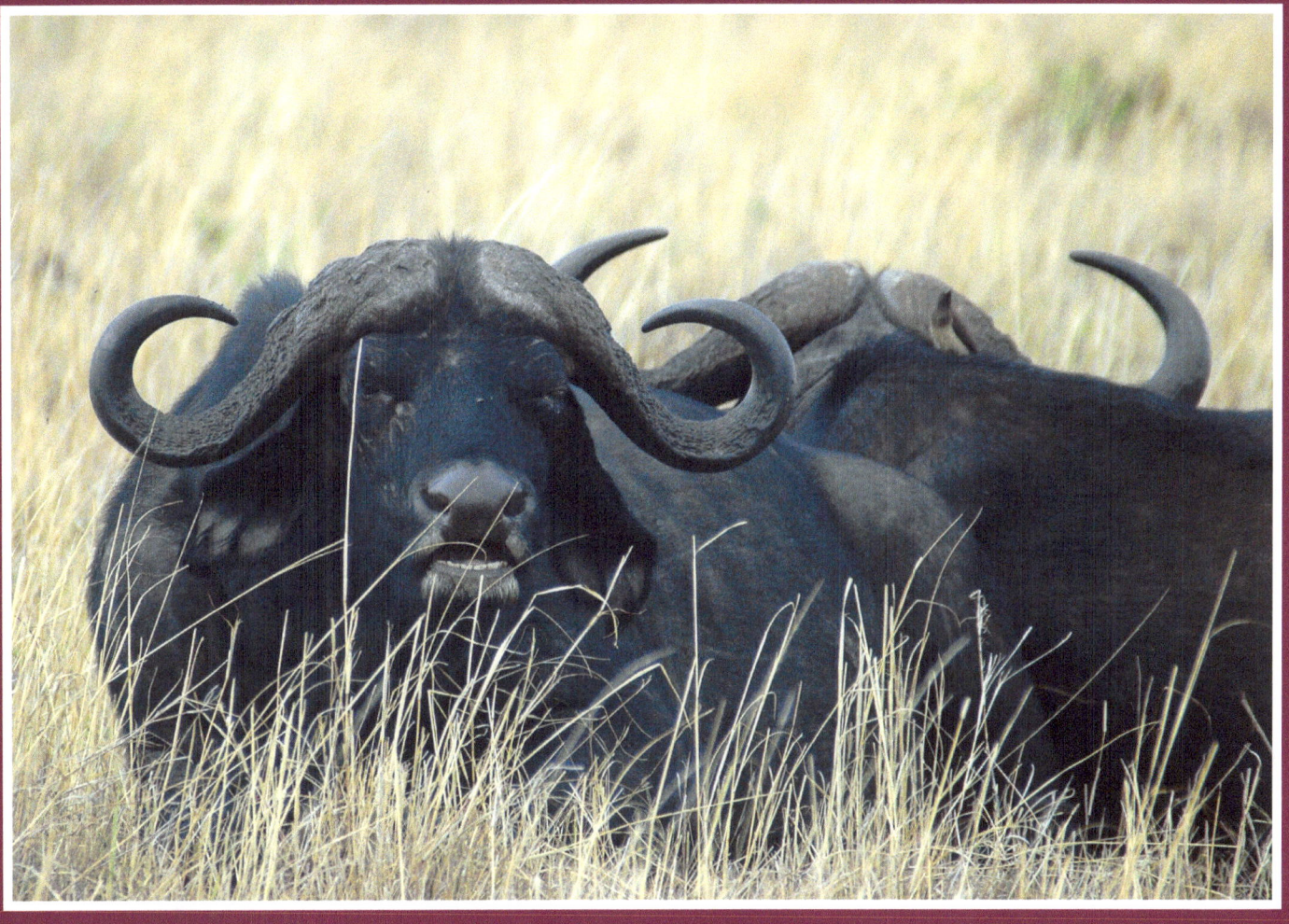

Cape Buffalo

岬水牛	Buffle	Kaffernbüffel	Cape Buffalo	Búfalo	Cape Nyati
Chinese	French	German	Italian	Spanish	Swahili

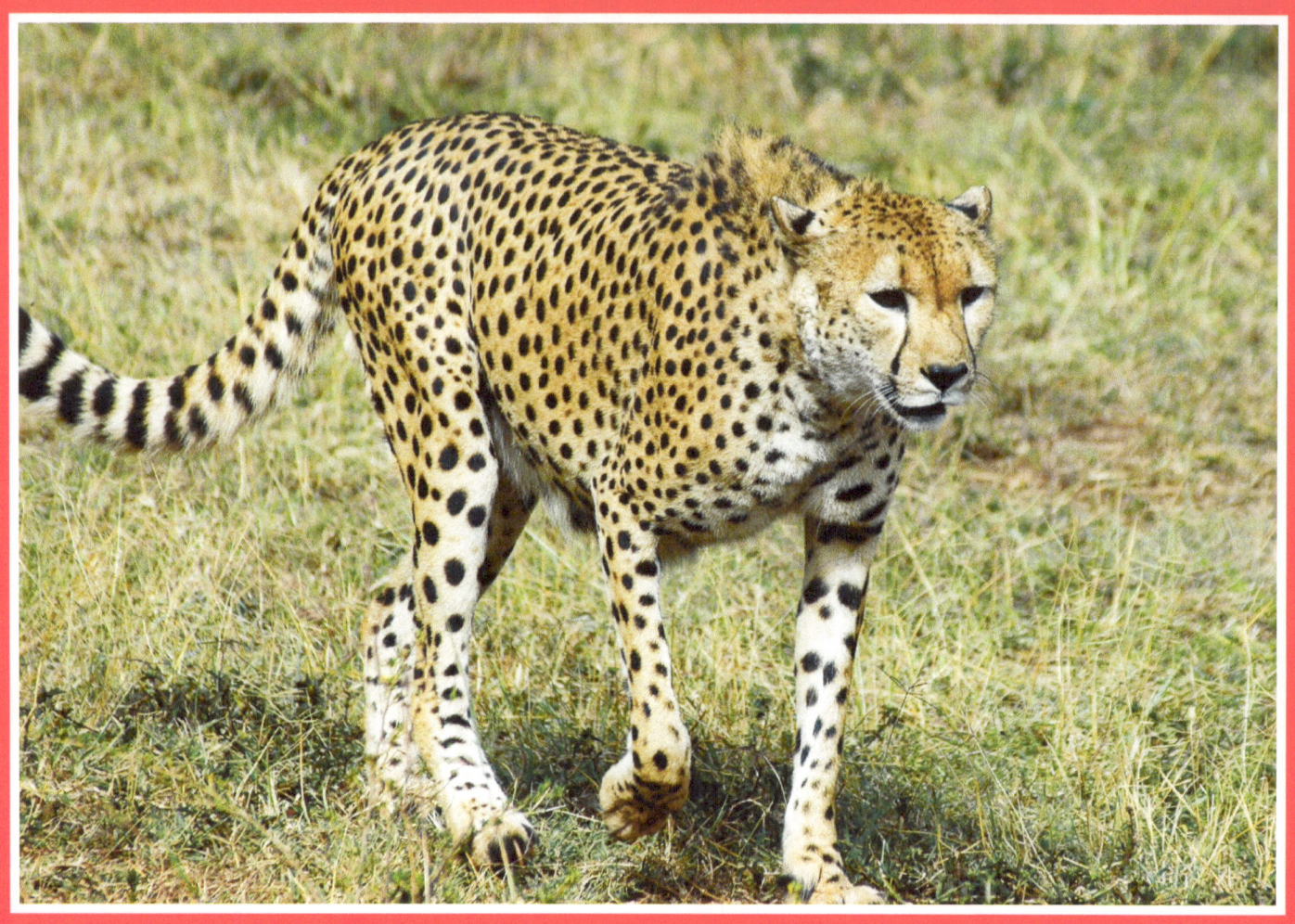

Cheetah

猎豹	Guépard	Gepard	Ghepardo	Guepardo	Duma
Chinese	French	German	Italian	Spanish	Swahili

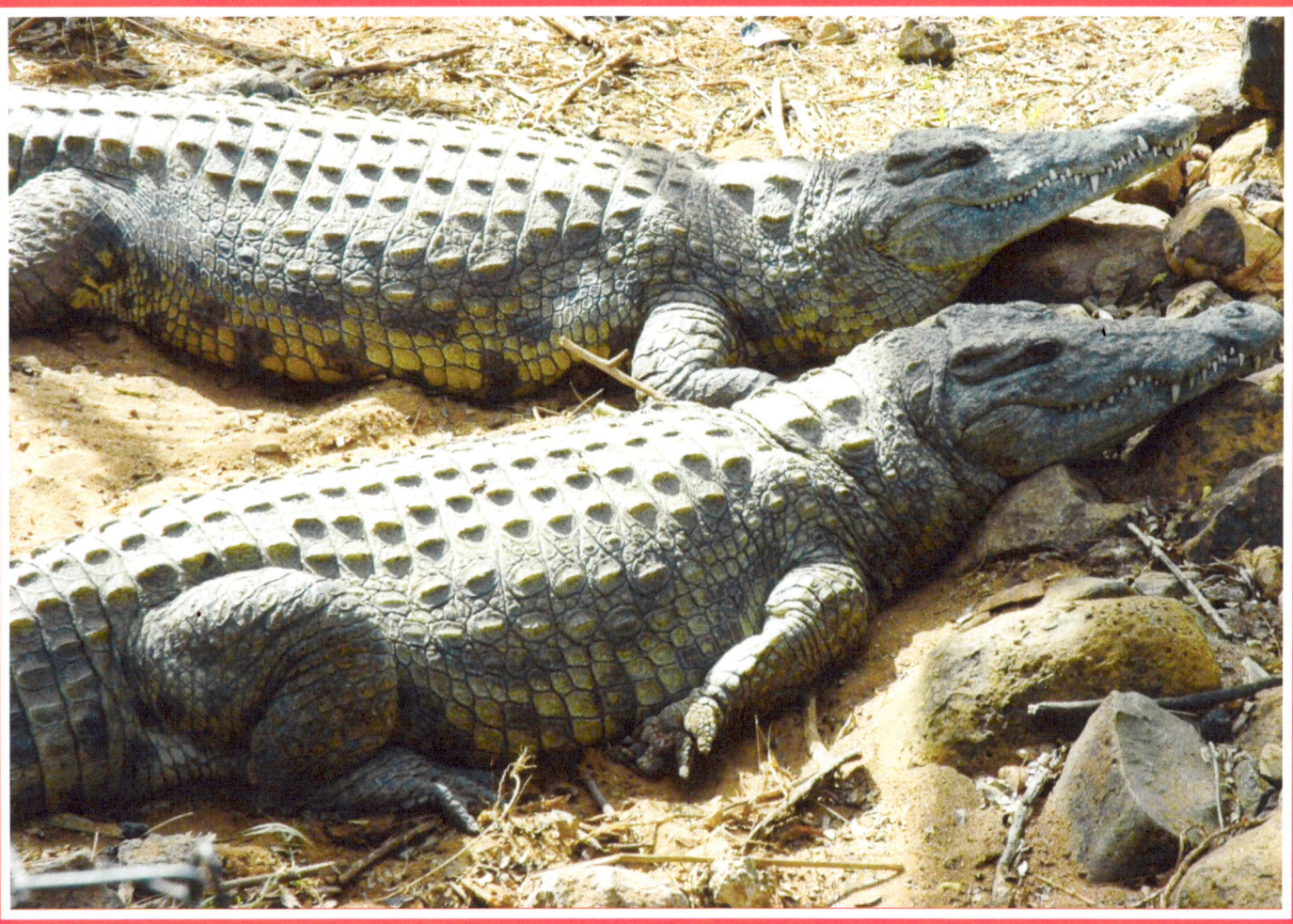

Crocodile

鳄鱼	Crocodile	Krokodil	Coccodrillo	Cocodrilo	Mamba
Chinese	French	German	Italian	Spanish	Swahili

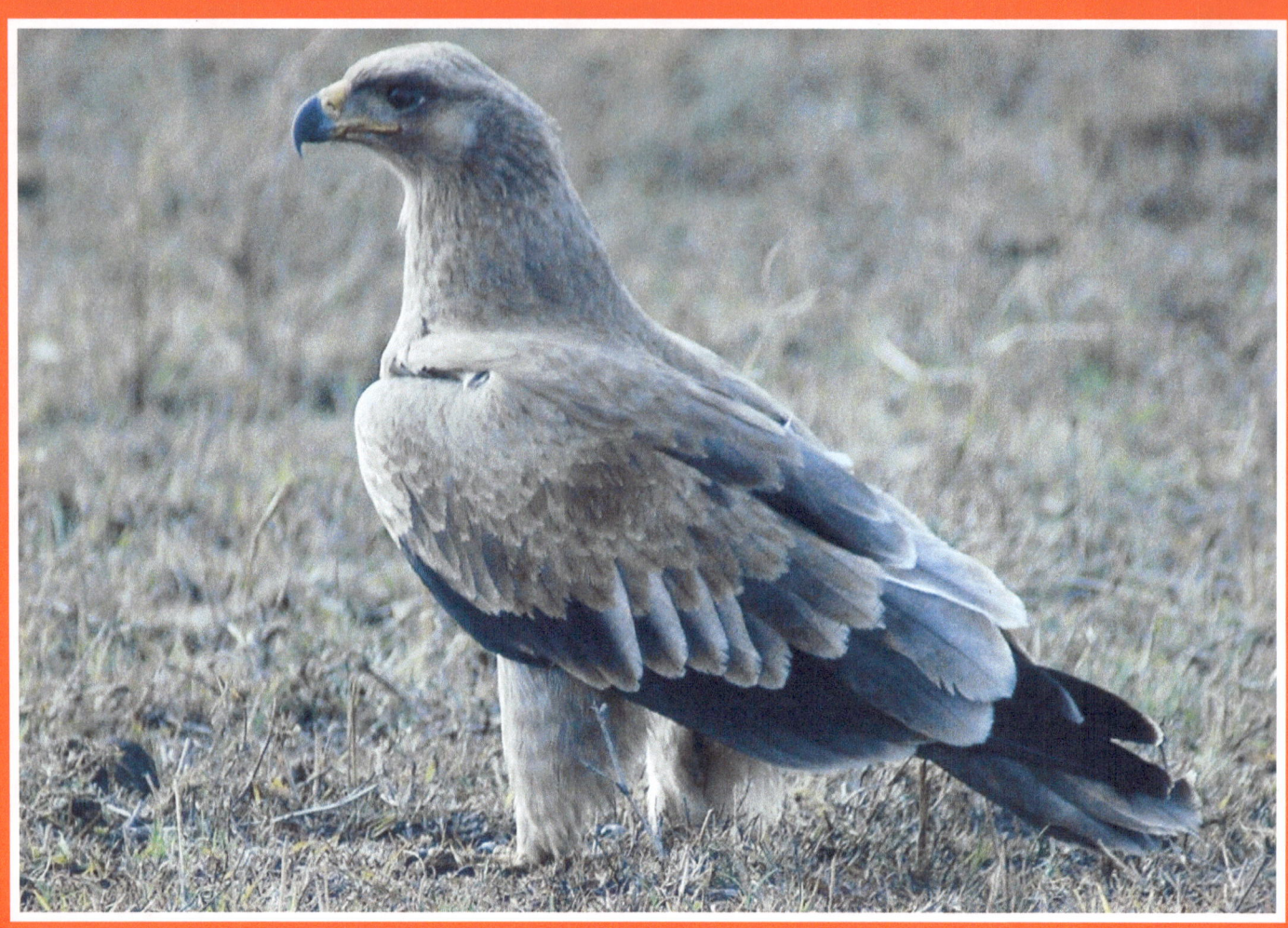

Eagle

老鹰	Aigle	Adler	Aquila	Àguila	Tai
Chinese	French	German	Italian	Spanish	Swahili

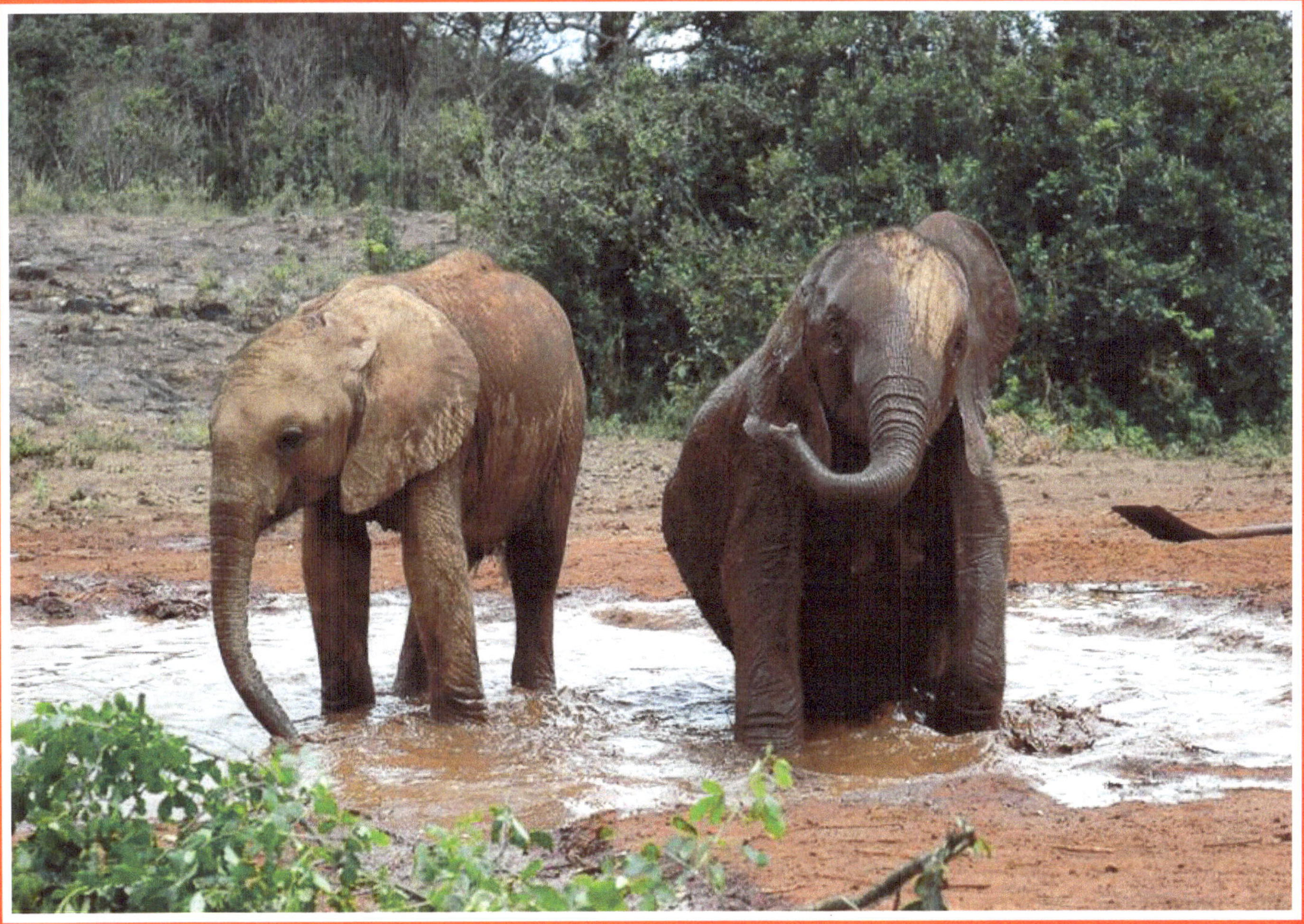

Elephant

象	Eléphant	Elefant	Elefante	Elefante	Tembo
Chinese	French	German	Italian	Spanish	Swahili

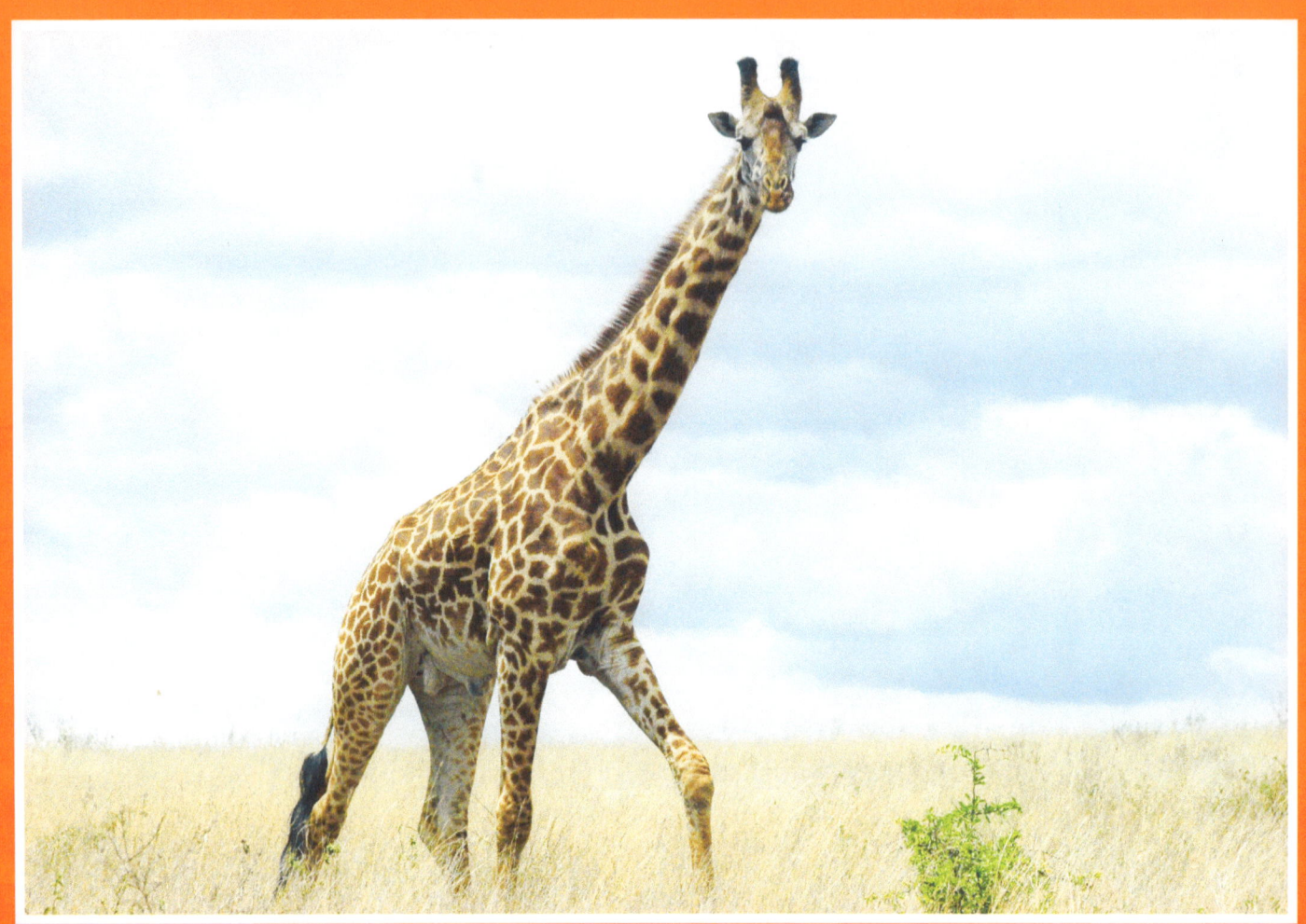

Giraffe

长颈鹿	Girafe	Giraffe	Giraffa	Jirafa	Twiga
Chinese	French	German	Italian	Spanish	Swahili

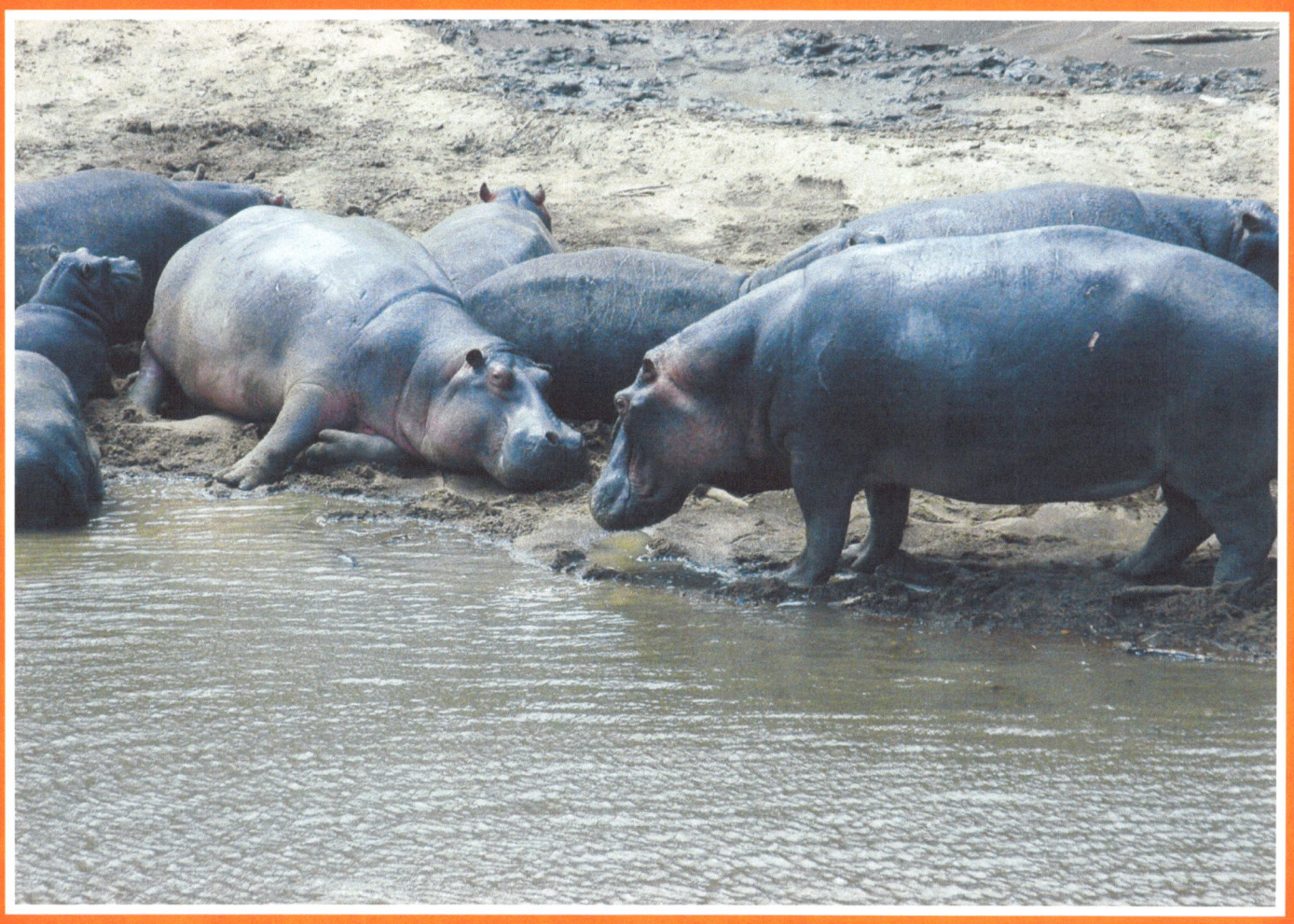

Hippopotamus

河马   **Hippopotame**   **Nilpferd**   **Hippopotami**   **Hipopótamo**   **Kiboko**

Chinese   French   German   Italian   Spanish   Swahili

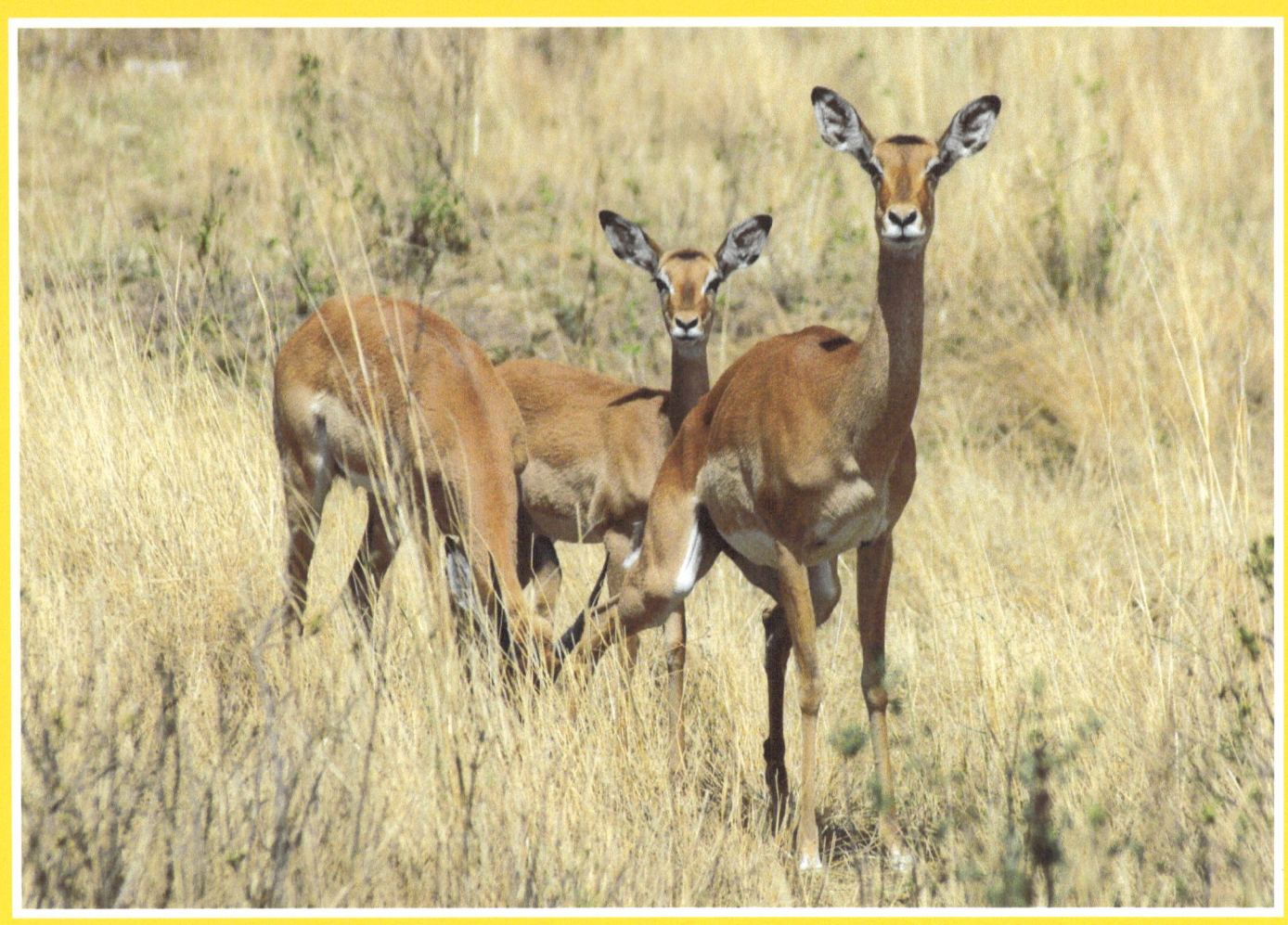

Impala

黑斑羚	Impala	Impala	Impala	Impala	Swala Pala
Chinese	French	German	Italian	Spanish	Swahili

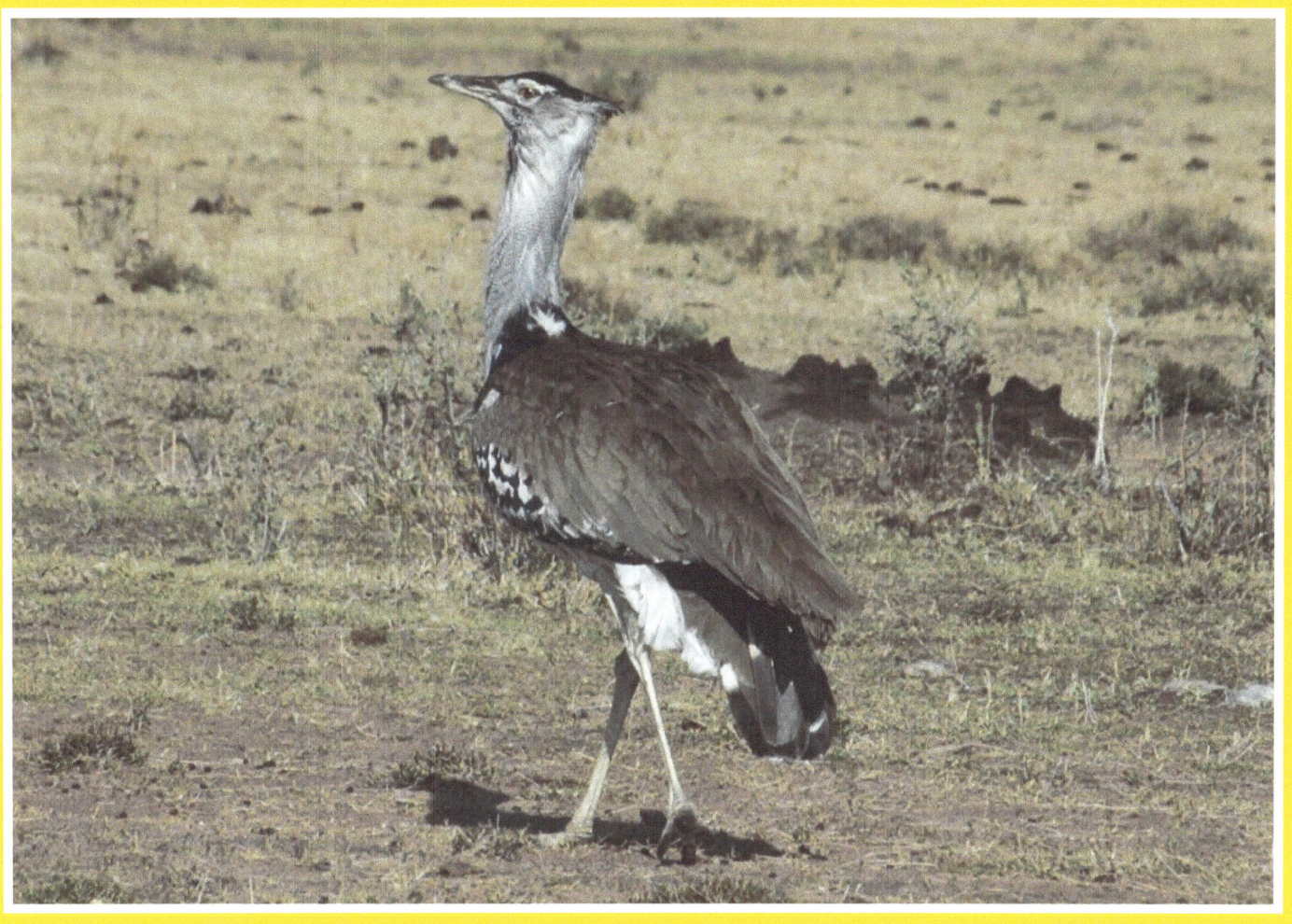

Kori Bustard

灰颈鹭鸨	Kori Bustard	Kori Bustard	Koria Bustard	Kori avutarda	Kori Bustard
Chinese	French	German	Italian	Spanish	Swahili

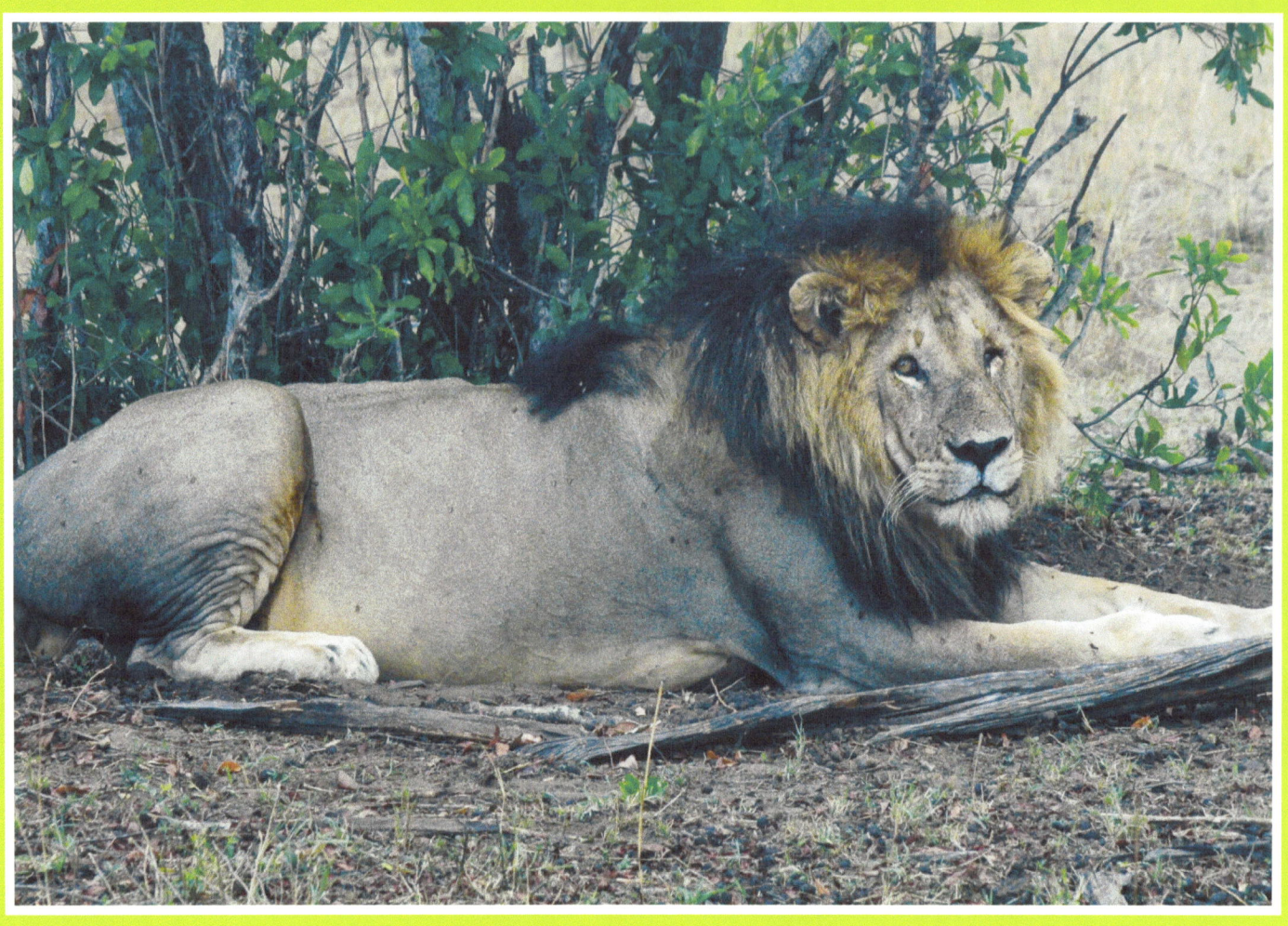

Lion

狮子	Lion	Löwe	Leone	León	Simba
Chinese	French	German	Italian	Spanish	Swahili

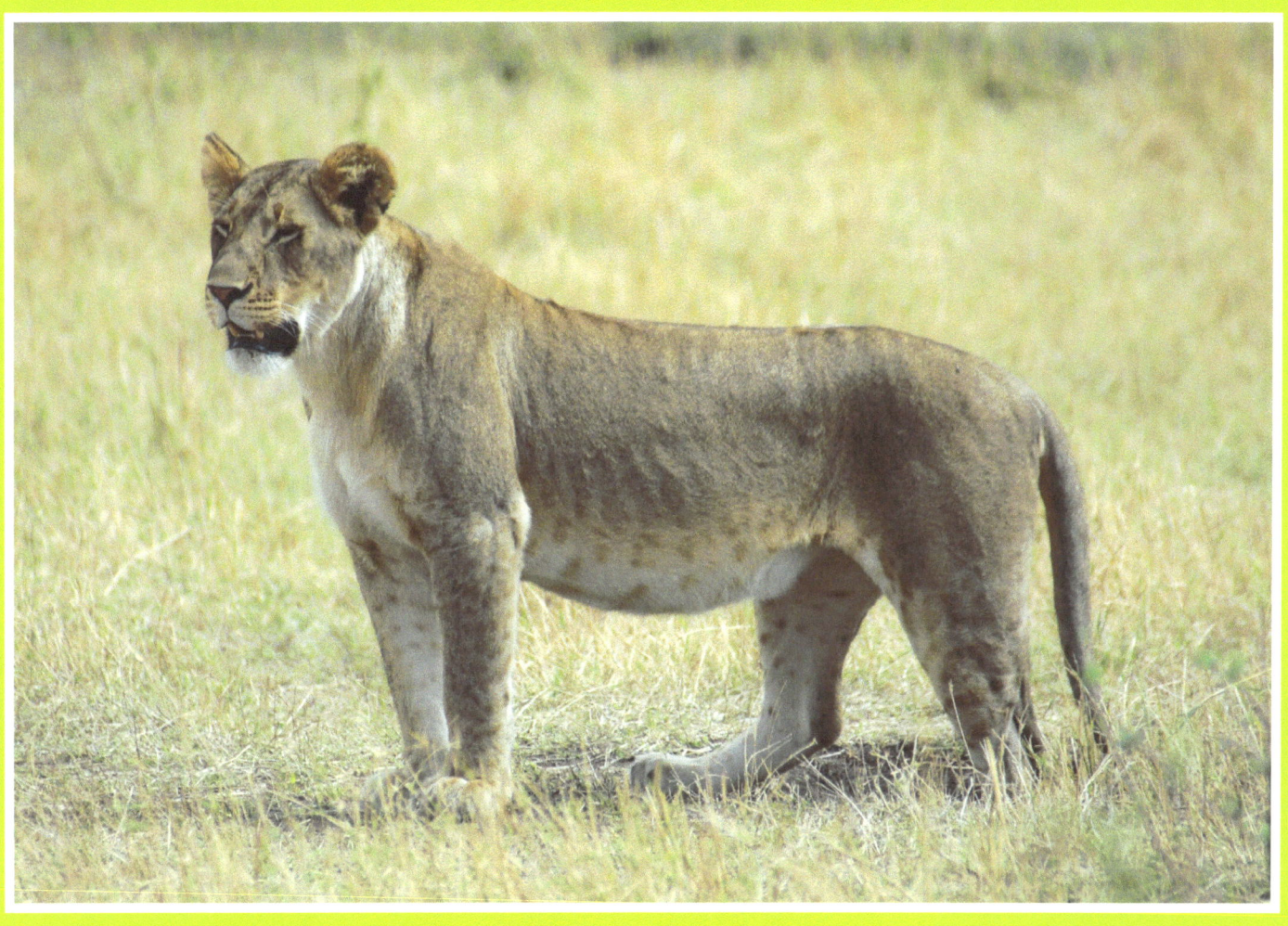

Lion

狮子	Lion	Löwe	Leone	León	Simba
Chinese	French	German	Italian	Spanish	Swahili

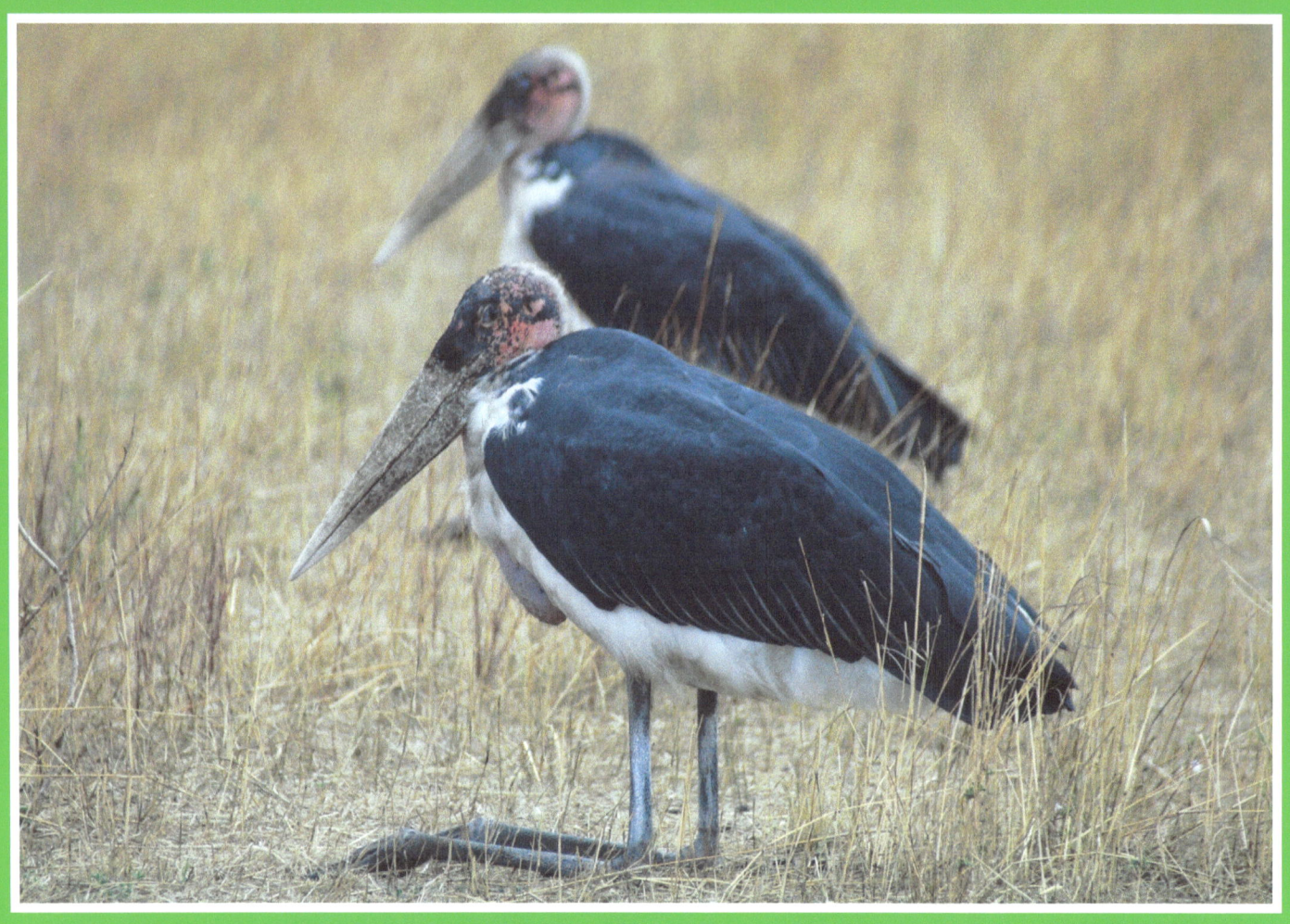

Marabou Stork

秃鹳	Marabou Cigogne	Marabou Storch	Cicogna Marabu	Cigüeña de marabú	Kongoti
Chinese	French	German	Italian	Spanish	Swahili

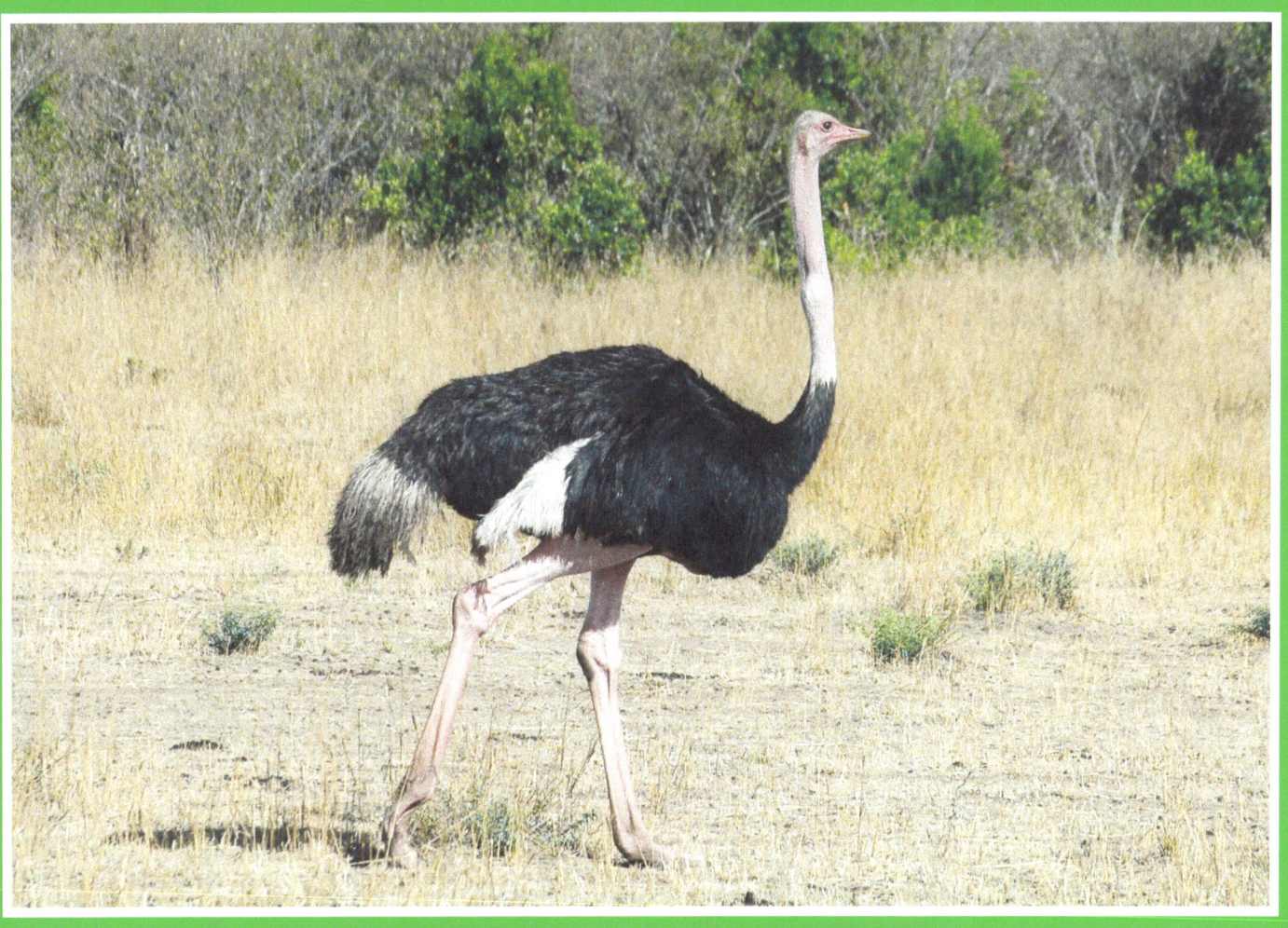

Ostrich

鸵鸟	Autruche	Strauss	Struzzo	Avestruz	Mbuni
Chinese	French	German	Italian	Spanish	Swahili

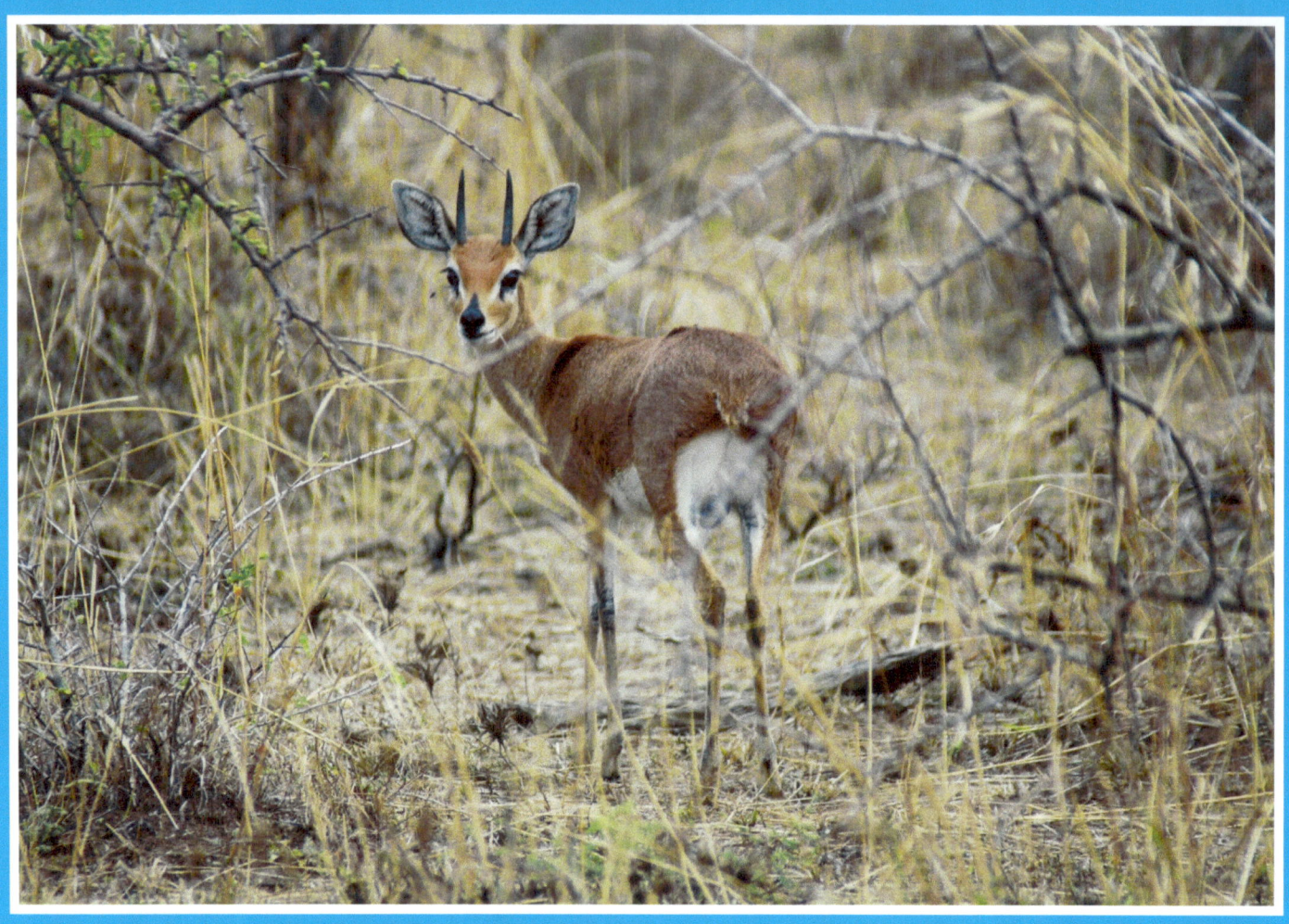

Steenbok

羚羊	Steenbok	Steinbok	Steenbok	Steenbok	Swala
Chinese	French	German	Italian	Spanish	Swahili

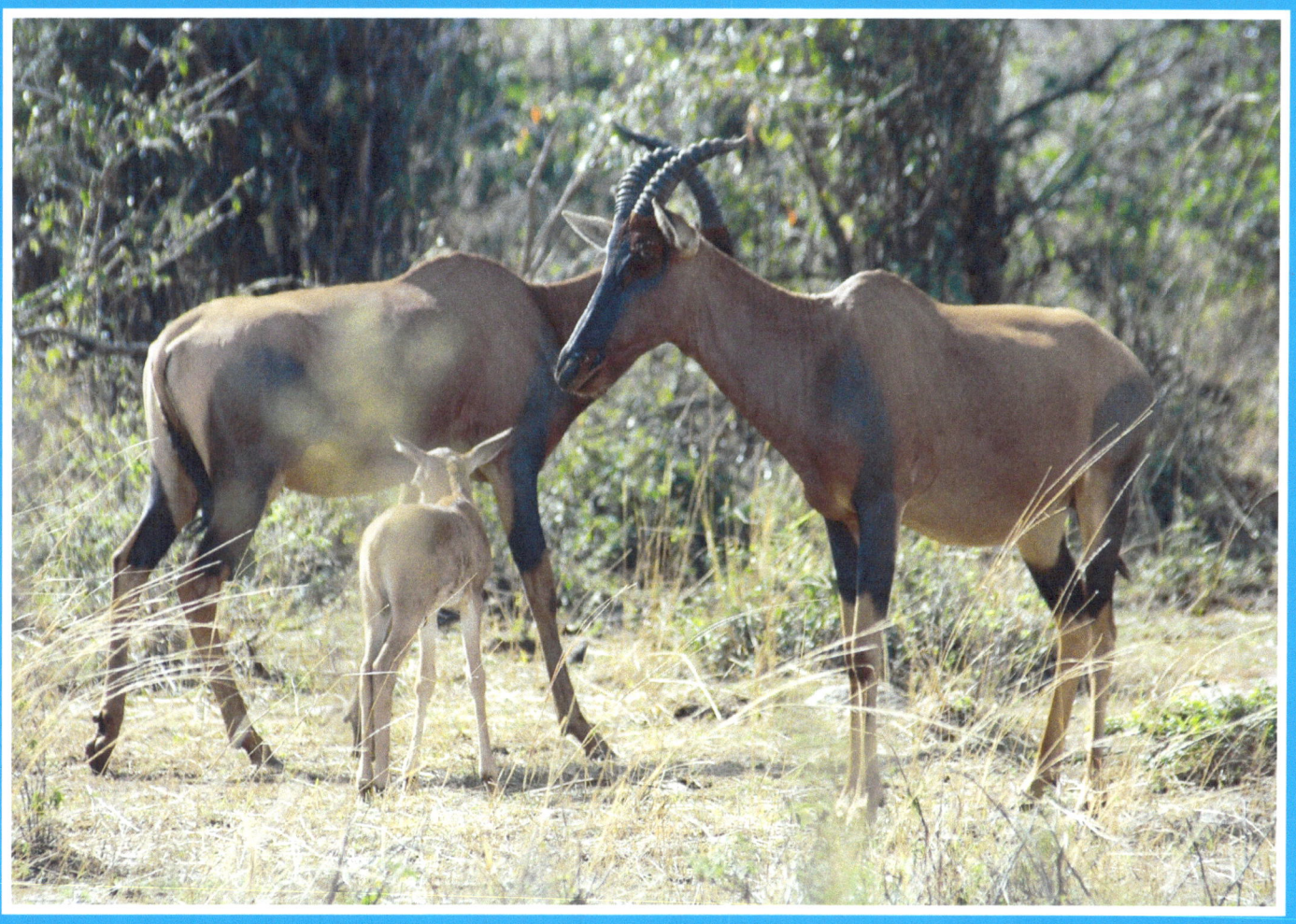

Topi

托皮	Topi	Tropenhelm	Topi	Topi	Nyamera
Chinese	French	German	Italian	Spanish	Swahili

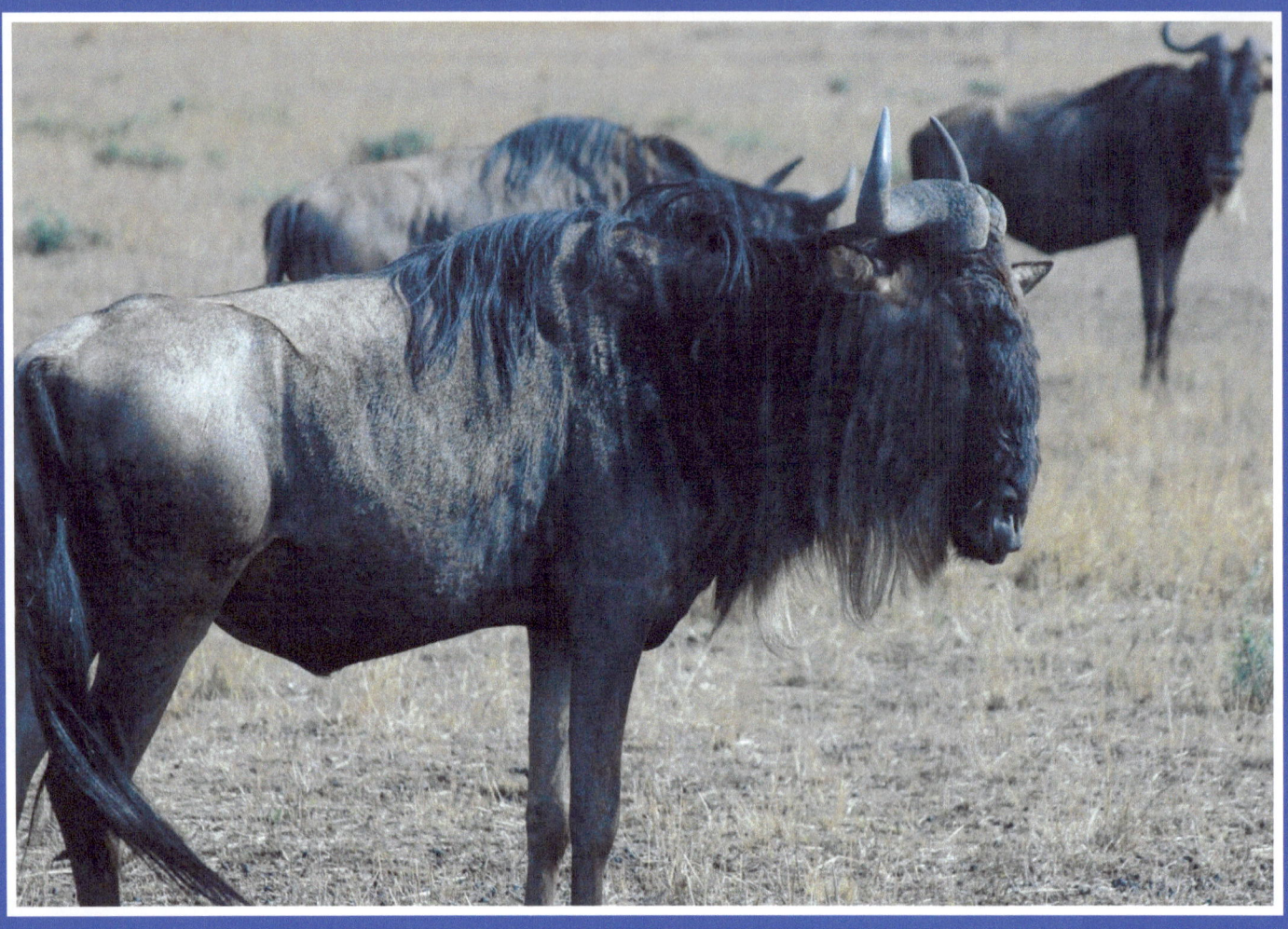

Wildebeest

牛羚	Gnou	Gnus	Gnu	Ńu	Nyumbu
Chinese	French	German	Italian	Spanish	Swahili

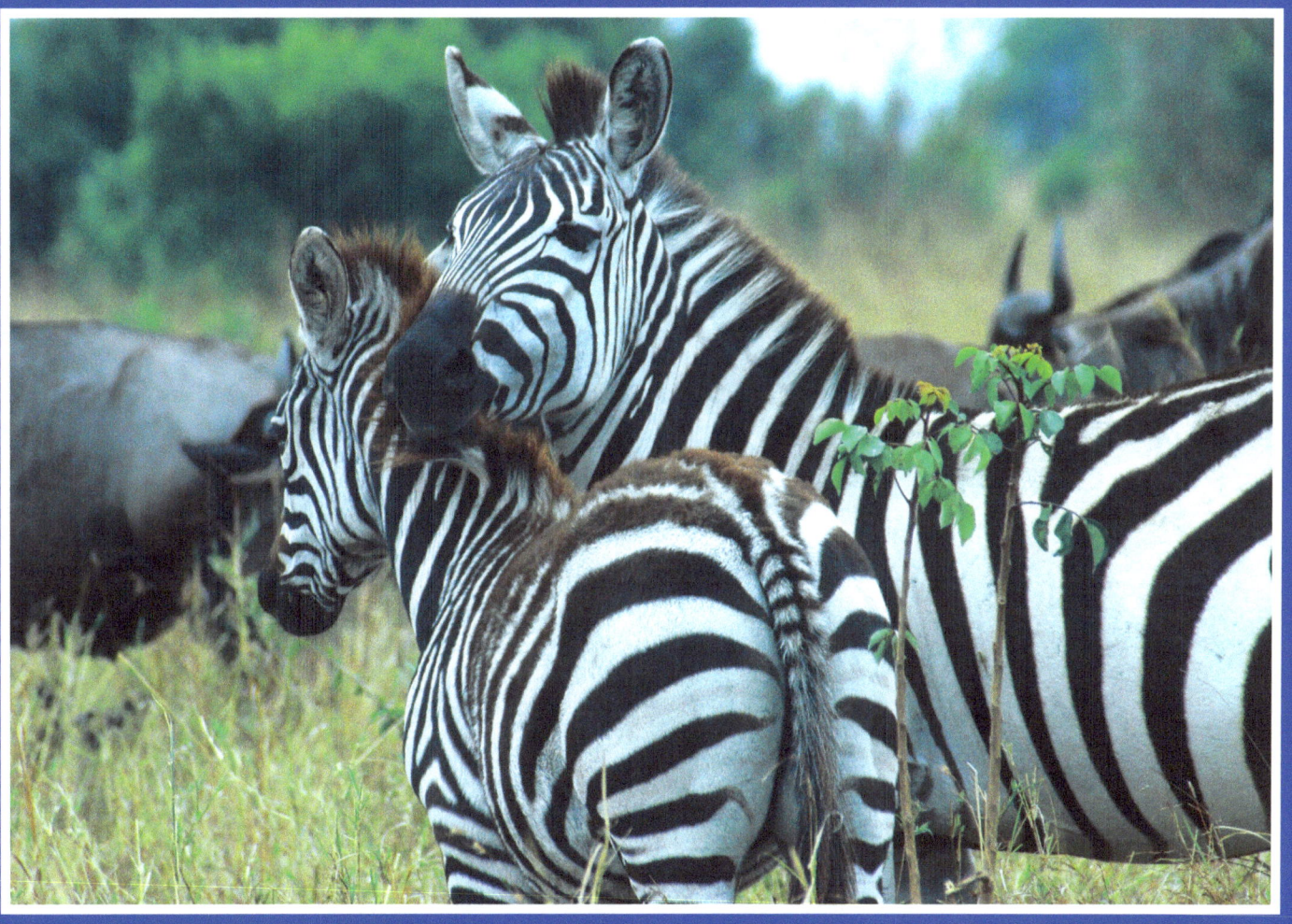

Zebra

斑马	Zèbre	Zebra	Zebra	Cebra	Punda Milia
Chinese	French	German	Italian	Spanish	Swahili

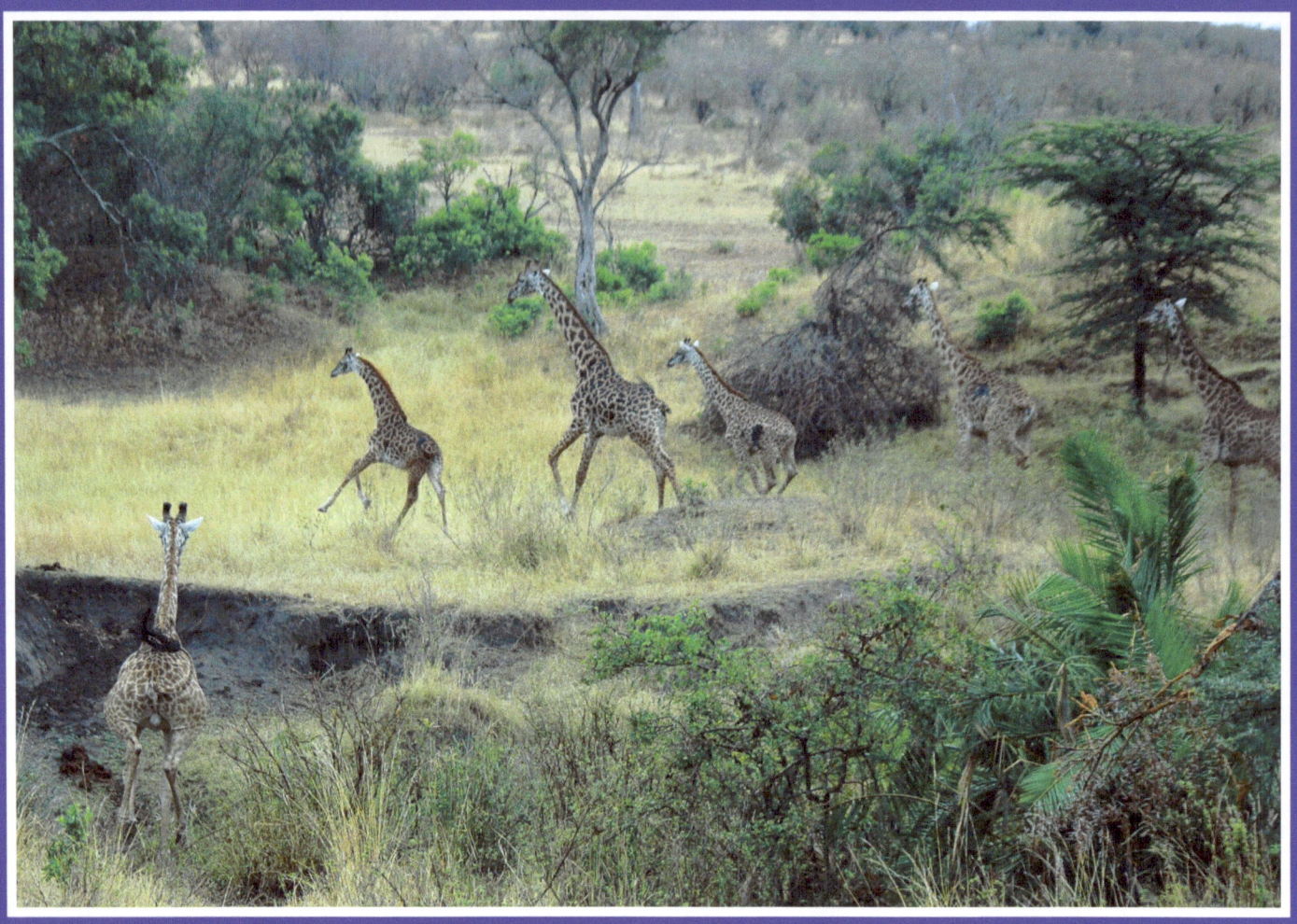

Good Bye

再见	Au revoir	Auf Wiedersehen	Arrivederci	Adiós	Kwa heri
Chinese	French	German	Italian	Spanish	Swahili

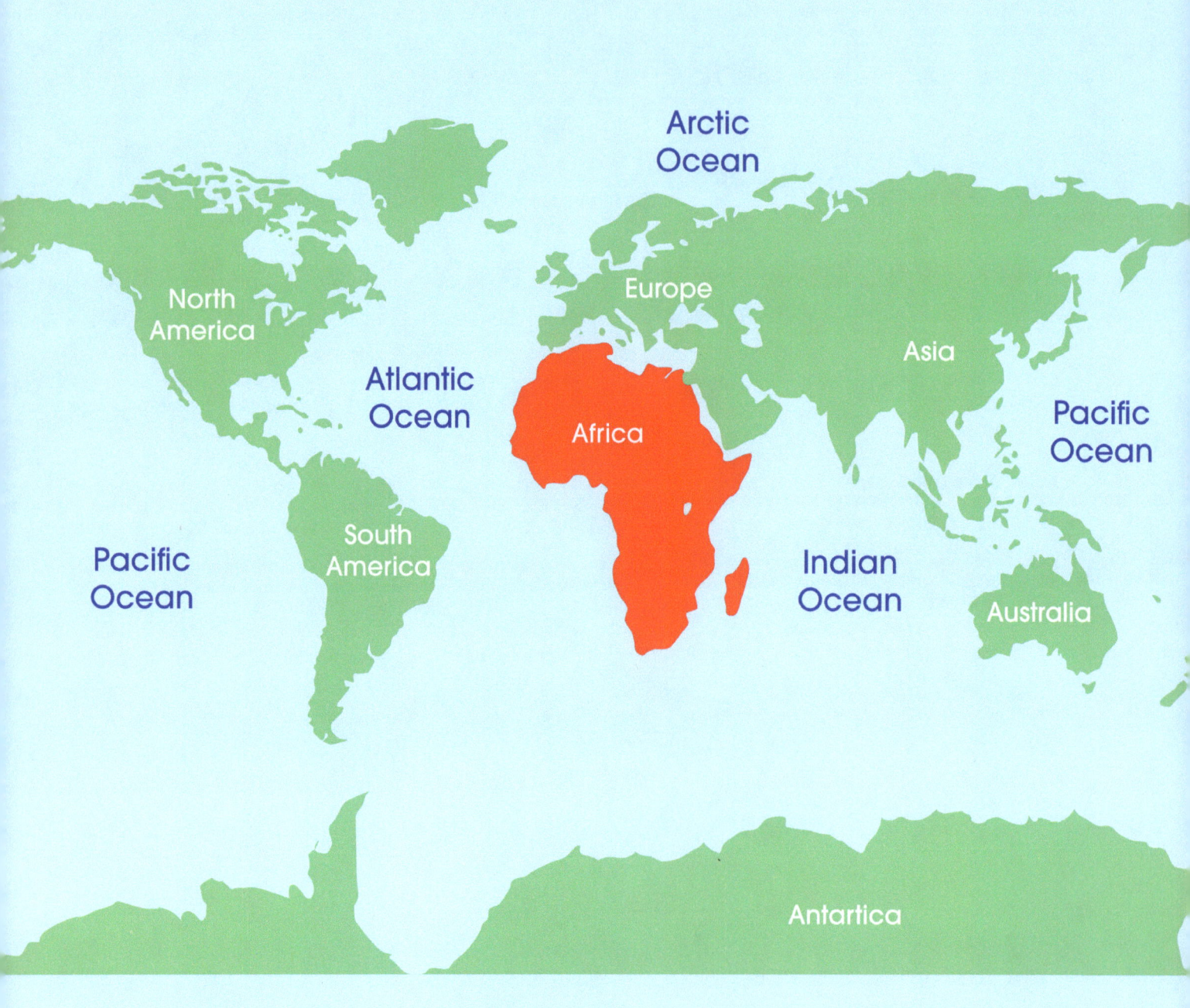

Arctic
Ocean

Europe

Asia

North
America

Atlantic
Ocean

Africa

Pacific
Ocean

Pacific
Ocean

South
America

Indian
Ocean

Australia

Antartica

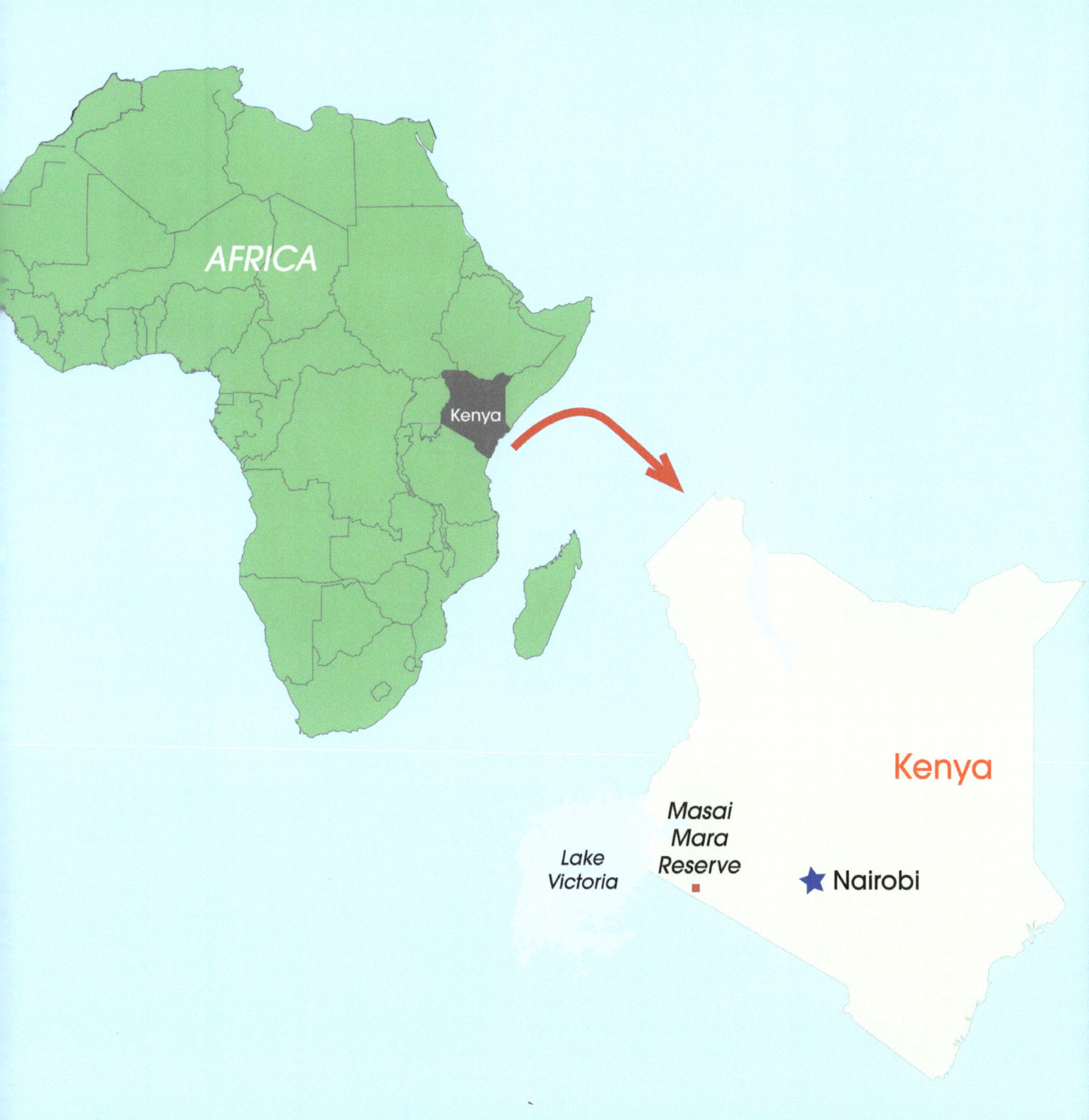

AFRICA

Kenya

Kenya

Lake
Victoria

Masai
Mara
Reserve

★ Nairobi

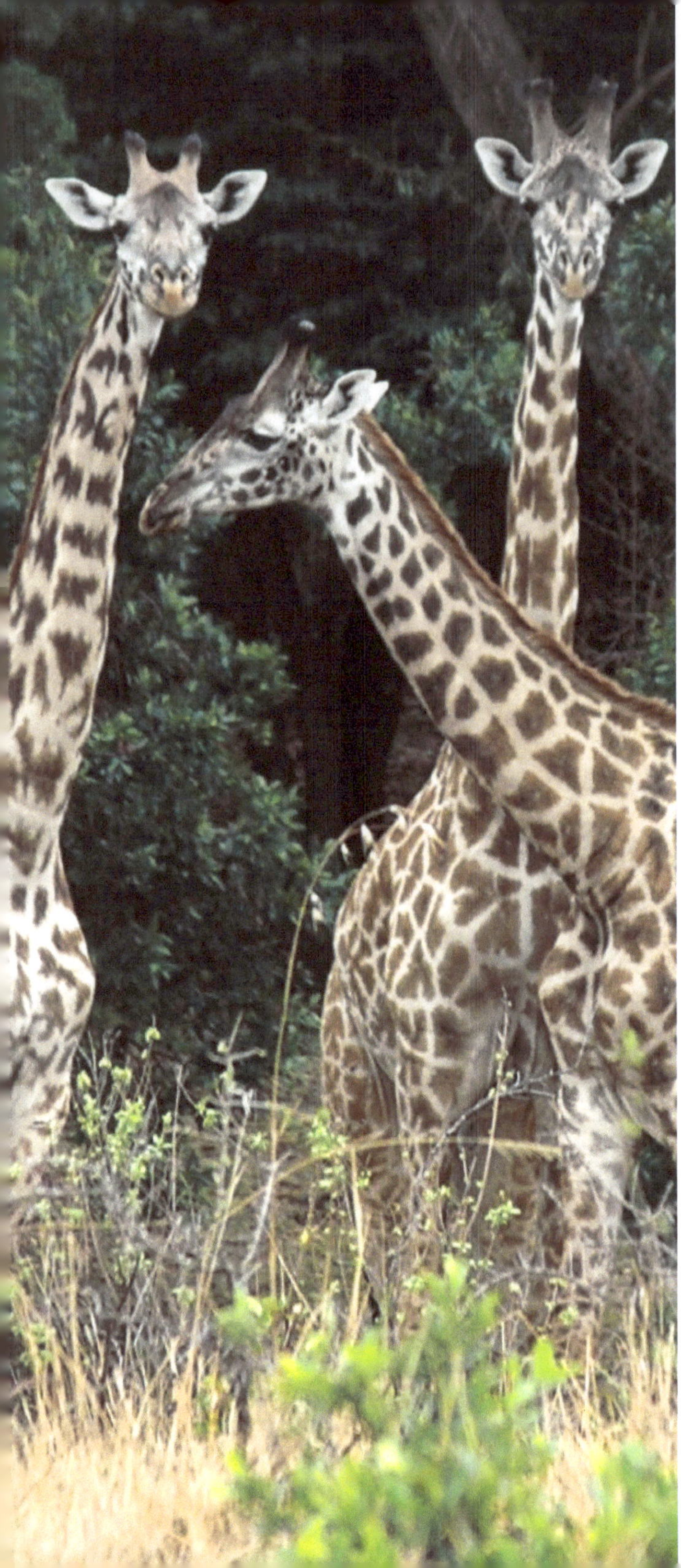

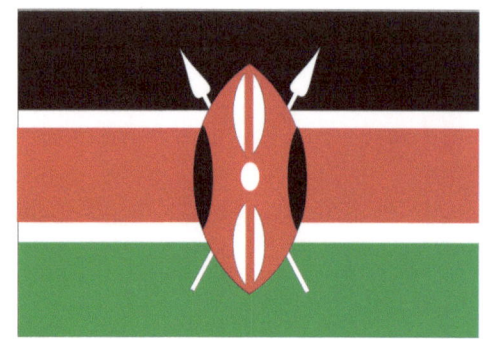

Ee Mungu Nguvu Yetu

Swahili lyrics

Ee Mungu nguvu yetu
Ilete baraka kwetu
Haki iwe ngao na mlinzi
Natukae na undugo
Amani na uhuru
Raha tupate na ustawi.

Amkeni ndugu zetu
Tufanye sote bidii
Nasi tujitoe kwa nguvu
Nchi yetu ya Kenya
Tunayoipenda
Tuwe tayari kuilinda

Natujenge taifa letu
Ee, ndio wajibu wetu
Kenya istahili heshima
Tuungane mikono
Pamoja kazini
Kila siku tuwe na shukrani

Oh God Our Strength

English translation

O God of all creation
Bless this our land and nation
Justice be our shield and defender
May we dwell in unity
Peace and liberty
Plenty be found within our borders.

Let one and all arise
With hearts both strong and true
Service be our earnest endeavour
And our homeland of Kenya
Heritage of splendour
Firm may we stand to defend

Let all with one accord
In common bond united
Build this our nation together
And the glory of Kenya
The fruit of our labour
Fill every heart with thanksgiving.

www.ingramcontent.com/pod-product-compliance
Lightning Source LLC
Chambersburg PA
CBHW050424180526

45159CB00005B/2398